Monetary Policy
Generates Poverty

Unchecked it will be our

Nation's Ruin

Richard D. Skillen, M.D

"You believe in things that you don't understand"

Stevie Wonder

"A people can only sink lower without a dependable store

of value. Currency debauchery is the *sole* source of U.S.

decline and decadence- just as it has been in every society

of recorded history"

Harry L. Schultz

Capitalism is to

Made in the United States of America

what

expansionary monetary policy is to

Made in Foreign Country

ABSTRACT

The financial stability of poor people has been in a continual decline since the 1950s, and this decline is a result of Federal Reserve Bank policy. This pamphlet tells us why and how this decline began, why it must end, and what we must do to end it.

Let's close our eyes, open our imaginations and visit 1954. In Claremont, New Hampshire, a city of some 13,000 residents, the downtown shopping district is anchored by MH Fishman, JJ Newbery, FW Woolworth, IGA, A+P, Montgomery Ward, and locally owned Houghton and Simonds, and is studded with dozens of smaller stores. On Friday nights, the district is bustling with activity, and being there then is as much a social event as it is a chance to do one's shopping. The minimum wage is $.75 an hour, and minimum wage workers are able to maintain households, make ends meet, and save for the future. Families of modest means are seeing their children graduate from the University of New Hampshire with little or no indebtedness. An 800 square foot home costs $6,500. The monthly mortgage payment is $35.15, and the annual property taxes are $90. A four room, heated apartment with hot water is $12 weekly. Another four-room apartment, this one newly renovated, is $8 weekly. A five-room apartment, with a garage, is $42 monthly. A rebuilt Electrolux vacuum cleaner, with seven attachments plus a sprayer, is $12.50. The home demonstration is free. A first-class stamp costs three cents. The doughnut shop at South and Pleasant offers plain doughnuts at three cents each, and filled doughnuts at five cents each. Blue collar workers own cottages on Crescent Lake, and in the summer old Evinrude motors pull skiers on the lake's inviting waters. The 1950s were affordable, and goods and services would have become even more affordable, but the Federal Reserve Bank intervened and kept that from happening.

After the Great Depression we were much concerned that another severe economic downturn might occur if some activist management of the economy was not put in place. The Great Depression began in 1929, and between 1929 and 1933 the money supply fell by 25%, prices fell by 25%, and the unemployment rate rose from 3.2% to 25%. The Federal Reserve Bank controls the size of the nation's money supply, and the size of the money supply is the key factor in determining prices. Increases in the money supply lead to higher prices, and shrinkage of the money supply leads to lower prices. Thinking that falling prices worsened the Depression, the Federal Reserve Bank adopted as a goal that prices will increase each year. Another way of defining this goal is that the dollar will weaken a bit each year, that the dollar will have less purchasing power each year than it had the year before. The manner by which the Federal Reserve Bank accomplishes this goal is termed expansionary monetary policy (the terms expansionary monetary policy and monetary policy are interchangeable. It is appropriate that there is not a policy intended to shrink the economy). This policy is felt to keep consumer spending high, employment full, and the national income in an endless climb. The Federal Reserve Bank assumed, mistakenly so, that everyone in the economy will benefit from the policy, and that the policy will be free of any adverse effect. The policy was established in the 1950s, and has been in continual use since then. Its establishment marked the beginning of the endless decline in the welfare of poor people. The policy has never received a careful reconsideration.

Economists see an economy as being homogenous, when it really is not. Any large economy has features that are in stark contrast to one another. Some sectors are advancing, while others are declining. Prices in advancing industries will rise, while prices in declining industries may fall. Workers in advancing industries can take pay increases that exceed the general increase in prices, while workers in declining industries may have to take a reduction in wages in order to keep their jobs. By not recognizing this, by not recognizing the economy's heterogeneity, our leaders cannot see the differing effects that rising prices have on the people. The policy's continual increase in prices accentuates the divergence of wealth and poverty. It favors those blessed to be employed in and invested in advancing industry jobs and opportunities, while it condemns those trapped in declining industry jobs. This is the basis for the rich getting richer and the poor poorer. Because monetary policy is practiced in that terrible laboratory called the real world, the declining industry effect is inescapable. The poor will continue to get poorer until the expansionary part of monetary policy is abandoned.

In 1954 our nation was poised for emergence of the most favorable economic era in history. Increases in efficiency (productivity) result in lower prices, and our economy has seen innumerable increases in efficiency this past half century. It will not be a surprise when history sees the last half of the 20th century as having been visited by more efficiency enhancements than any other five-decade time period. When boards are replaced by plywood, plaster by sheetrock, hammers by nail guns, and hand saws by power saws, efficiency increases; and these increases allow carpenters to build houses at reduced cost. Similarly, the internet allows capitalists and individuals to pay bills and transact business at reduced cost. New materials handling equipment has the same effect. The list goes on and on, and across all sectors of the economy. Capitalists never stop their search for more economical ways to produce and distribute their goods and services. This they do in order to maximize their profits, but in so doing they gift the people with products that are more and more affordable. In fact, capitalists, the ones so many of us like to blame for our economic woes, keep a paradoxical lid on prices while they line their pockets, and this lid remains in place until it is removed by monetary policy.

Our economy in 2018 is a pitiful substitute for what it would have been if the affordability of the 1950s had been allowed to survive. Monetary policy has, to borrow Peggy Noonan's words, "...tanked a great nation's economy." More recently, Ms. Noonan, of the Wall Street Journal, stated: "We are as a nation in a moment of real peril." Morris Dees, of the Southern Poverty Law Center, would readily agree. Monetary policy caused the dollar to lose 86% of its purchasing power between 1954 and 2004; and the decline continues. If the net effect of policy from 2004 to 2054 replicates that of 1954 to 2004 the dollar will lose another 86% of its purchasing power. It will then take one dollar to purchase what could have been purchased in 1954 for less than two pennies (a penny and change). How can such a policy strengthen a nation and help it to long endure? How can it give a poor person – or anyone – optimism for the days ahead?

From its origination in the 1950s, expansionary monetary policy has been nothing more than a treatment trial – a test run. The policy's continual and endless weakening of the dollar is damaging the economy. The trial is a failure, and the policy should be discontinued. There is not one unambiguous benefit of this weakening, while its devastating impact on the lives of poor people is without question. The policy also brings into question the stability and solvency of Medicare and Social Security. The policy funded the increase in stock prices that led to the high-tech selloff in 2000, and it funded the increase in real estate prices that led to our economic downturn in 2007-2008. The policy is why the more than helpful Five and Dimes are gone, and why the Dollar Stores' days are numbered. The main ingredient in the 1960s War on Poverty was expansionary monetary policy, making it easy to understand why that war was a failure, and why it has come to appear that war is being waged against the poor people we want to uplift. *There is no possible way that our leaders have our nation headed for a favorable destination.* The Federal Reserve Bank should abandon the policy of weakening the dollar, and accept the strengthening of the dollar that capitalists willingly, though unwittingly, provide. *Only this* can convert our economy's long deterioration into a true and lasting recovery. Yes, the solution, expansionary monetary policy, is the problem. Once the solution is abandoned the problem will end, and the economy will effect its own gradual but unending recovery. Let the people reclaim the favorable journey that was taken from them six decades ago. Let there be a renaissance of affordability. Let the healing begin.

References

15 U.S.C. Sec. 1021. et al, 1946. *The Employment Act of 1946*

A Class of Distinction. The Wall Street Journal 26 May 1996: A7

A Look at the Global One Percent. The Wall Street Journal 9 Mar. 2012 *[New York, NY]*: A15. Print.

As *Rich-Poor Gap Widens in the U.S., Class Mobility Stalls.* The Wall Street Journal 13 May 2005 [New York, NY]

Bade, Robin, and Michael Parkin. *Foundations of Economics.* Fourth Edition. Boston: Pearson, 2009

Balsley, Howard L. *Readings in Economics Doctrines.* Paterson, New Jersey: Adams and Company, 1961

Counsel of Economic Advisors. Economic Indicators. October 1995.

Divided by Income: The Gap Widening Between Richest and Poorest in Wealthy Connecticut. Hartford Courant 6 Aug. 2001 [Hartford, CT].

The Economist. *Singing at the Underclass.* Dec. 23rd 1995 – January 5th 1996 page 34

Fisher, Irving. *The Money Illusion.* New York City: Adelphi Company, 1928

Fisher, Irving. *The Purchasing Power of Money*. New York: Macmillan, 1911

"For U.S. Universities, a Growing Wealth Gap." *The Wall Street Journal* 1 Dec. 2007 *[New York, New York]*. Print.

Friedman, Milton, and Anna Jacobson Schwartz. *A Monetary History of the United States, 1867-1960*. Princeton: Princeton University Press, 1963

Friedman, Milton. *An Economist's Protest*. Glen Ridge, N.J.: Thomas Horton and Daughters, 1975

Friedman, Milton. *Capitalism and Freedom*. Chicago: The University of Chicago Press, 1962

Hansen, Alvin H. *Economic Issues of the 1960s*. New York: McGraw Hill Book Company, 1960

Hawtrey, Sir Ralph George. *Currency and Credit*. London: Longmans, Green and Company, 1919

Income-Inequality Gap Widens. The Wall Street Journal 12 Oct. 2007: A3.

Jevons, W. Stanley. *Investigation in Currency and Finance*. Second Edition. London: Macmillan, 1909

Keynes, John M., *the General Theory of Employment, Interest and Money*. Cambridge, England: Macmillan Cambridge University Press, 1936.

Krugman, Paul. *The Age of Diminished Expectations*. Cambridge, Massachusetts: The MIT Press, 1995 page 29

Malinowski, Bronislaw. *Magic, Science, and Religion and Other Essays*. Glencoe: Free Press, 1948

Marshall, Alfred. *Principles of Economics*. London: The Macmillan Company, 1920

Mill, John Stuart. *Principles of Political Economy*. New York: Appleton – Century – Crofts, Inc., 1878

Mitchell, B.R. International Historical Statistics: The Americas. 1750-1988, NYC Stockton Press 1993

Murray, Charles A,. *Losing Ground: American Social Policy*. 1950-1980, [New York, NY]: Basic Books 1984

Nock, A. *Our Enemy, The State*. San Francisco: Fox & Wilkes, 1994

Noonan, Peggy. *Declarations.* The Wall Street Journal 15 Oct. 2011 [New York, NY]: A15.

Noonan, Peggy. *Declarations.* The Wall Street Journal 5 May 2012 [New York, NY]: A15

Phillips, A.W., et al, *The Relation Between Unemployment, and the Rate of Change of Money Wage Rates in The United Kingdom, 1861-1957*. Economica (1958): 283-300.

Politics and People. The Wall Street Journal 26 December 1996: A7

Rich Hold Greater Concentration of the Wealth. News and Observer 30 Sep. 1997 [Raleigh, NC].

Smith, Adam. *An Inquiry into the Nature and Causes of the Wealth of Nations*. Chicago: Methuen & Co., Ltd., 1976. Print.

'Smith, Adam.' *Supermoney*. [New York, NY]: Random House, 1972.

Top Earners' Pay Is Seen Eroding Social Security. The Wall Street Journal 21 July 2009: C1 [New York, NY]

Whitman, D. *The Rise of the 'Hyper-Poor'*. US News and World Report. Volume 109 Issue 15. October 15, 1990. Pg. 40

Who wins in the new economy? The Wall Street Journal 27, 06 2001; B1

Appendix

The War on Poverty would have been a success were it not for the fact that our elected and appointed leaders on and about Capitol Hill sent the wrong troops. They sent the Federal Reserve Bank when they should have sent the capitalists. We have seen how expansionary monetary policy drives more and more people into poverty each year. Declining prices have the opposite effect. Declining prices lift people from poverty. Each year of declining prices sees more and more people able to make ends meet. This effect of declining prices ameliorates the problems of declining industries. Unaffordable goods and services gradually become affordable. Yes, our nation *was* poised for emergence of the most favorable economic era in history, and capitalism would have driven that process. The higher prices of monetary policy should be replaced with capitalism's gifts of lower prices. We must abandon current policy; only after that abandonment will poor people be once again able to save for the future

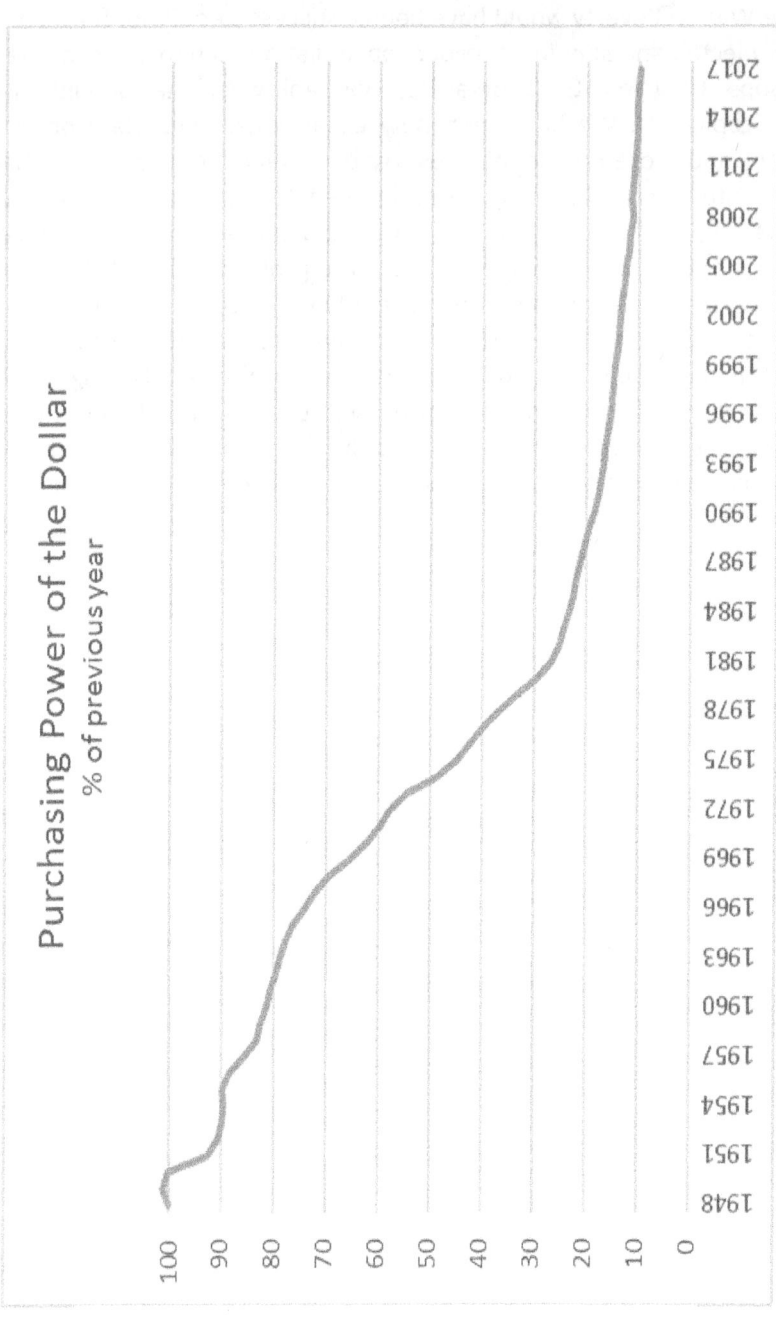

Source: Bureau of Labor Statistics Year 1948 = 100

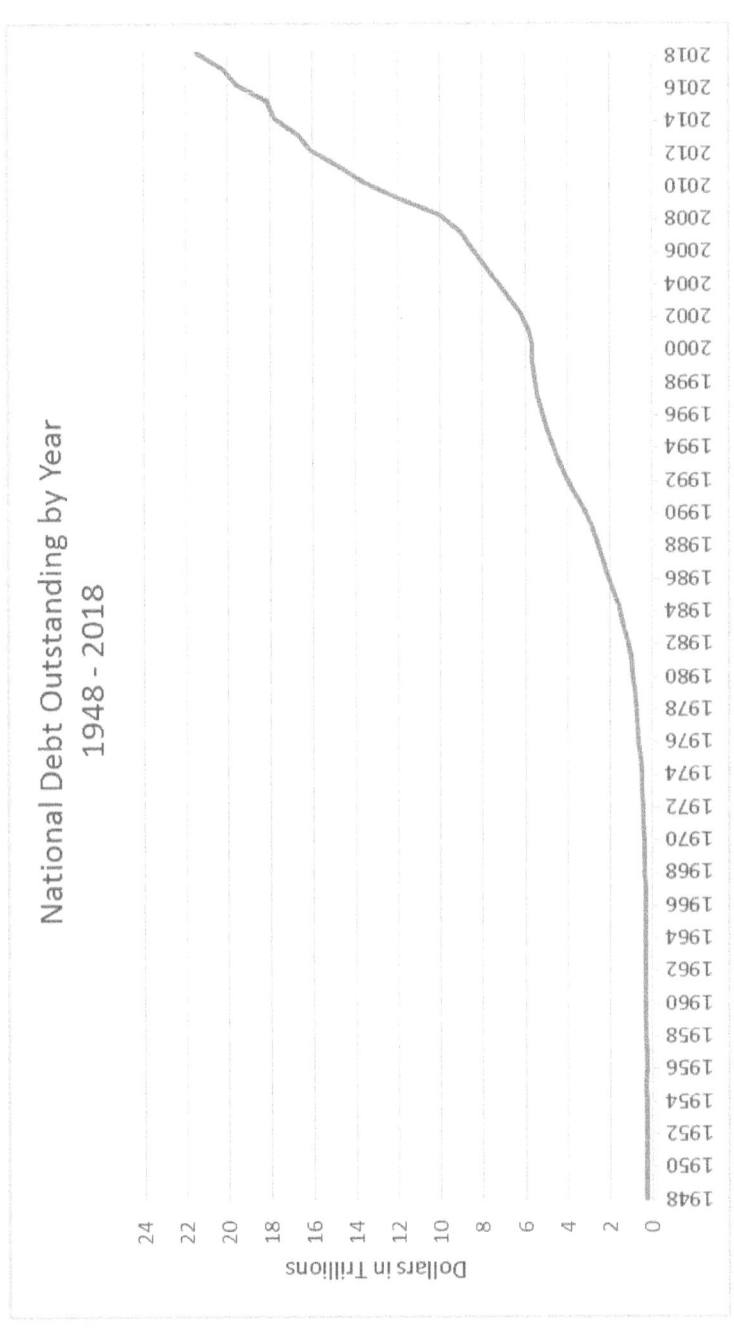

Source: TreasuryDirect.gov Historical Debt Outstanding

The Federal Reserve Bank Chairmen

Chairmen	Date of term
Charles S. Hamlin	Aug. 10, 1914 – Aug. 9, 1916
W.P.G. Harding	Aug. 10, 1916 – Aug. 9, 1922
Daniel R. Crissinger	May 1, 1923 – Sept. 15, 1927
Roy A. Young	Oct. 4, 1927 – Aug. 31, 1930
Eugene Meyer	Sept. 16, 1930 – May 10, 1933
Eugene R. Black	May 19, 1933 – Aug. 15, 1934
Marriner S. Eccles	Nov. 15, 1934 – Jan. 31, 1948
Thomas B. McCabe	Apr. 15, 1948 – Mar. 31, 1951
Wm. McC. Martin, Jr	Apr. 2, 1951 – Jan. 31, 1970
Arthur F. Burns	Feb. 1, 1970 – Jan. 31, 1978
G. William Miller	Mar. 8, 1978 – Aug. 6, 1979
Paul A. Volcker	Aug. 6, 1979 – Aug. 11, 1987
Alan Greenspan	Aug. 11, 1987 – Jan. 31, 2006
Ben S. Bernanke	Feb. 1, 2006 – Jan. 31, 2014
Janet L. Yellen	Feb. 3, 2014 – Feb. 3, 2018
Jerome Powell	Feb. 5, 2018 –

About the Author

Dr. Skillen attended schools in Claremont, N.H., and graduated from Stevens High School in 1963. He graduated from the University of New Hampshire in 1967, the University of Vermont College of Medicine in 1971, and completed his internship at New Hanover Memorial Hospital in Wilmington, North Carolina from July 1, 1971 – June 30, 1972. He received a Master of Arts in Economics from North Carolina State University in 1986. Dr. Skillen and his family reside in Garner, N.C.

www.ingramcontent.com/pod-product-compliance
Lightning Source LLC
Chambersburg PA
CBHW051206170526
45158CB00005B/1850